The FACES *of* NAMI

Mark McClintock

Paperback-Press
an imprint of A & S Publishing
A & S Holmes, Inc.

ISBN: 0692380388
ISBN-13: 978-0692380383

DEDICATION

I wish to thank our Joplin, MO. NAMI chapter for sharing with me these last 3 years laughter, tears, and the reality of having a mental illness. I truly have been inspired, humbled, and very much encouraged by your strength you've shown in dealing with the challenges every one of us faces with mental illnesses. I'm grateful that you've allowed me to record your stories in this book!

I also want to thank my wife Rose for understanding the "less than perfect" tendencies we who have mental illnesses carry with us. She has given of herself on my behalf, and I admire her for doing just that.

My sister Mary Ellen comes to mind when I think of giving a "thank you". I can always call her for encouragement, and I'll often use Mary as a "sounding-board" while she makes my low days be better days!

TABLE OF CONTENTS

About NAMI
(NATIONAL ALLIANCE ON MENTAL ILLNESS)

NAMI, the National Alliance for Mental Illness, is our nation's largest organization devoted to dispelling the myths and stigma associated with mental illnesses. NAMI strives to educate people with mental illnesses about ways to live their lives with meaning and hope!

NAMI has over 1,000 chapters in the U.S.A. which gather together weekly to share their coping skills and encourage one another in their journeys with mental illness. These NAMI groups prove to be a lifesaver for people who live day to day with mental illness and also helps their families, too.

ACKNOWLEDGMENTS

I want to recognize all the NAMI groups everywhere for reaching people in the biggest needs of their lives, and giving them the hope that only NAMI can present. NAMI support groups with unlimited information are an awesome witness toward healing and helping folks find their road toward recovery!

NAMI chapters are an oasis for thousands of people that are looking for a better quality of life and find just that in NAMI.

I wish to give a great big ***thank you*** to Shawn, our friend and graphic artist! Shawn, your cover design is creative and very inspirational. Thank you forever!

FORWARD

I have found our Joplin NAMI group to be even more than a really great group of people. We are folks that give support to each other during our challenging periods in our lives. We truly care about each other and know how to best serve each person's struggles.

I sure wish that NAMI (National Alliance for Mental Illness), would've been part of my efforts for recovery back years ago, when I was first diagnosed with mental illness!

Actually, the people mentioned in these pages, (in my opinion), are angels sent from God to bless each other! Every one of them have shown real courage and character when faced with the intimidating presence of mental illness. We know best how things can "go south" quickly, for whatever reason it occurs.

My reason for writing this book is to portray the message of HOPE!! Tomorrow shall be "a brighter day!" Every person who has a mental illness has the opportunity to work like crazy to find a psychiatrist or nurse practitioner for medicines, a counselor to re-group regularly with, a support group, (why not NAMI?) and a church or spiritual group for uplifting our souls.

Recovery is a beautiful word, and it's something each and every one of us must strive for one precious day at a time!

Thanks to all of you, and may God bless you,

Mark McClintock

SHERYL

My mental illness first appeared during the post-partum period following my first daughter's birth. My girl was 9 months old when one day my patience was shot and I "just lost it!" I shook my little girl violently and then dropped her to the floor. I called my mom and told her what had happened. She responded, "Bring her over here now!" My mom called my family doctor, and made an immediate appointment. Our doctor diagnosed me as having post-partum depression and prescribed Prozac which gave me some relief.

I've fought depression since December of 1988. While in high school I experienced anxiety at some serious levels. Starting in the year 2000 'til 2010, I had panic attacks of huge proportions. I was working at Scholastic Books during this time. My doctor prescribed Wellbutrin which was a great medication until I discovered the price tag! I quit my job at Scholastic Books in 2010 and the panic attacks got less frequent.

I began seeing a nurse practitioner in Joplin who was giving me too many pills. I secretly began saving the pills I didn't use and made a secret plan inside myself to take them in a suicide effort. One heavy, dark Sunday morning I went to church, but all the people appeared to be millions of miles away-surely not in my painful world. I went home and tried to end my life by taking 70 pills. My mom and step dad came to my house and called 911, and the paramedics revived me, as I'd passed out.

Following this period of time, my husband and I divorced and I moved in with my mom and step dad.

I also made a very good friend at the chicken processing plant where we worked. Today we remain close. My work is physically hard, but it's location takes me near my 2 girls and their families, and it provides me with insurance coverage.

I have begun attending NAMI meetings with my step dad on Tuesday nights-it's opened a whole new way of thinking for me! I now can relate to other people that struggle with the same type of problems I have. This has never been the case, and it's really a refreshing experience!

MARISSA FORT

I was born Sept. 26, 1986. I was sexually abused from age 6 'til age 12 by 2 cousins. Whenever I turned 13, I confronted them and that put an end to it. Around this age, I began taking medications for anxiety and depression.

When I was 15, while on a vacation in Las Vegas, I was raped while my friend watched.(some "friend") At this stage in my teen years, I became quite promiscuous, running with a fast, unpredictable crowd.

I became pregnant at 18, but my boyfriend beat me up so badly that I lost the child. It was at this point in my life that I vowed never to drink alcohol again, and I've held fast to that promise!

One bright area that happened when I turned 19 was my meeting my fiancé Gary. I got pregnant again, but lost the baby to a miscarriage at 3 months into the pregnancy

I pretty much just "survived" my 20's, and at age 26 I was diagnosed as having 'borderline personality disorder." The therapy I received from my counselor proved to be invaluable!

The NAMI support group has really meant a lot to my progress with living with mental illness. The love, acceptance, and absence of judgment I've received from the members of our NAMI family truly has been a blessing!

IRENE MARSHALL

I was four when I suffered my first trauma. I was told my parents were sending me to live with relatives. By the time I was eight I had developed all my symptoms including a food disorder.

I remember the depression, the feeling different until twelve when I lost weight and got caught up in physical attention from boys. That is how I lived my life...no goals, just addiction switched from food to boys.

At age 14 I had my first panic attack and spent weeks in bed. The family took me to the doctor who said, "She does not have bronchitis but is having difficulty breathing because she has anxiety disorder."

My mother threw a pan of mashed potatoes at me that night and said, "How dare you do this to me." I had lived in four different places with other people at this point and never with her. My mother blamed me for having a disorder. I was supposed to take it all and be okay.

It took years of therapy and then 12 steps to become a person.

At 20 I married a man I did not love, nor him me. I lived a lie and continued to get more depressed and have more panic. The doctors kept putting me on Valium and I barely could leave the house. I had my Valium and food and just wanted to be left alone. I did try to volunteer and go to church, but my existence was bare...this was from 20 to 30.

I made the decision to come to MO. based on my husband's inability to support us in NY. He was drinking and getting into trouble.

At age 24 I had panic attacks so bad that I ran out of a Planned Parenthood clinic on a 10 degree night in paper clothes. I was so scared of being in there, and then I knew I needed help.

My cousin said, "You better get help for this!" I found the local mental health clinic and began therapy. I am so grateful to this day. It was a long trip to get healthy, (about 19 years), but when I got it, I got it.

After moving to MO, I was gravely depressed and went to the hospital. It was my decision and they put me on anti-depressants for the first time.

Leaving my home state threw me into another anxiety period with major depression. I was 31 at the time. When I was 38, my husband of 20 years left me in his mid-life crisis and here I was in Joplin, still sad about not being home, and now sad about losing my family. This was trauma #2.

This threw me into an episode of insanity which lasted 4 years. I picked up a book called, "Women Who Love Too Much". After reading it I got on my knees and pleaded with God to let me have this recovery and that I would do whatever the doctor, author of this book, said to do. The first thing that had to be done was to begin Al-Anon. I did on July 4, 1986, and my life was forever changed. Oh not in one night...I fought it like crazy and began 14 meetings a week with Al-Anon, AA, OA, NA, and Adult Children of Alcoholics. After four years I went into treatment for four months. That is where I re-learned how to think, how to act and not react, and how to be healthy in spite of my mental disorder...I was changed by the grace of God.

In 1991 I married my present husband, Doyle, who is a kind, hardworking man and we actually met in the treatment center. I was there for relationship addiction and all the other addictions.

I feel that the 12 steps is a cognitive learning recovery, which is why it worked for me. I believe I have some sort of personality disorder, and maybe bi-polar. I'm not sure as I have kept that to myself for my own reasons. I did well being treated for the depression/anxiety, with therapy and changing my way of living, thinking and benefiting from my 12 step recovery programs.

When I got well, and they did not think I would make it as they had never seen someone with such dependency needs as myself, but after four years the recovery people were amazed to see my recovery. I am still amazed and know only God could do for me what I could not do for myself.

Every day is an experience of re-training me there from negative to positive to gratitude, to peace etc, etc. Mental illness is not an easy road, but from my terrible childhood and the three traumas I lived through, I know it can be a better life in recovery, One Day at a Time.

I feel the first trauma was my parents sending me away at four years old and at that moment I never felt right again. Abandonment and PTSD immediately, and fear that stayed with me all my life,

The next trauma was leaving my home state that I truly loved, a totally foreign culture, a way of thinking and living right down to my ethnic background, to being an Italian, Catholic New York democrat in SW Missouri. That, I still deal with each and every day.

The third trauma was in 1984 when my husband left me, and I was again abandoned, and I was a stay-at-home mom that didn't know what to do. I turned to men and drinking until I found recovery, well not found it, I was led there by our loving God.

I am not cured, not by a long shot, but I do have peace, yes, I do have joy and, yes contentment. Not all day but hour by hour and more peace than not. Before recovery I had NO peace, and panic attacks, fear, dependency insecurity, low self-esteem, and no hope whatsoever. Today I live to pass it on. You see when on my knees back in 1986 after reading "Women Who Love Too Much", I told God "if you help me recover I will spend the rest of my life passing it on". I got recovery, and I am still passing it on wherever and whenever I can. Every day is a new opportunity to do the Lord's work!

Today I have NAMI and today I have hope, one day at a time.

A very grateful person,
Irene Marshall

IRENE'S COUSIN BILL

This is the story of my cousin Billy, a wonderful man. As a kid he was gentle and kind, though a bit mischievous. I giggle as I think of him roller skating on the streets of Brooklyn always scaring us younger ones. I was 2 years younger than Billy. As my story goes, you know I was afraid of everything.

Billy was the 1st grandchild and he was adored. He grew up in Brooklyn, New York knowing his plan from early on. He was accepted into Brooklyn Tech High School and then Polytech Institute. One had to be on the top of the list to get in. He did and he worked so hard for 9 years to get his Aeronautical Engineer degree. He received it at about 23 years old. He also married his young sweetheart at a wonderful wedding in Manhattan, New York. They were like a prince and princess at the wedding...both beautiful.

His mental illness was not apparent at this time. While growing up he showed signs here and there, like hiding in a closet and getting pleasure from scaring his younger sister. We now know this was part of the characteristics of his illness. These facts would later be shown when he became ill with the disease.

Our grandfather had paranoid schizophrenia and was a dangerous man. We all have a mental illness originating with him. He married his 1st cousin, our grandmother, and the disease began.

Bill began a prestigious career as an engineer at Bethlehem Steel in Bethlehem PA...he was only 23 years old and hired over many men older than he. This is where the stress was one thing too many that started his symptoms. The men didn't like him because of his age and coming in as a boss as they had been there for many years.

Bill was brilliant and of course all of this set him on his course for mental illness. He was ripe for it with the new marriage, graduation, new job, and new state he moved into.

The doctors said later on that if all the stressors had not occurred at one time he may not have become ill with his predisposed illness of schizophrenia.

His wife became pregnant and that was the last straw of pressures that finally ignited his illness. He began by feeling his car was bugged, and calling the police. He started hearing voices and feeling as if people were out to get him. He would pace the floors and behave in a manner that was not him but the illness taking him over.

They had to leave their home in Bethlehem and go back to Brooklyn where Bill moved in with his mom and dad, my aunt and uncle. There was no rhyme nor reason with his behavior...he became excited, fearful, and threatening. At one point this gentle young man attacked his mother and they came and put him in a strait jacket and took him for his 1st hospitalization. How sad this was. He no longer resembled in any way the wonderful young groom and graduate of just a couple of years ago. His very appearance began to change.

The only medication they had for him was Thorazine, and later on Mellaril. While in the hospital he escaped and went missing. They knew he had been in the house in Brooklyn, his folks' home, because some items of clothing were missing. I am not sure how he was found but he had been hiding in the mountains somewhere in the tri-state of New York, PA, or Jersey. Back to the hospital.

After a number of trips to the hospital, his wife divorcing him, and no hope, he went to his mom and dad's and stayed with them in Brooklyn. He was little more than a robot of fear. The television scared him as he thought they were talking to him...the cars honking horns or people moving their lips all became part of his paranoid delusions.

There was nothing left of that young man who had graduated a few years before, bright eyed, handsome and so kind and intelligent. Now he was pacing the floors mumbling back at the voices he heard all day long. He was terrified for a long time...His mom and dad didn't know what to do.

They had a simple life, his dad was a WW11 veteran and a hard worker, and his mom an everyday homemaker, wife and mom. What happened to their world...they were helpless.

After a few years Bill began to drink...he found the voices would lessen for long periods during each day and he increased his drinking by volumes. He took up smoking and ended up drinking a case of beer every other day. He was on disability now and lived with his parents and he used his money to supply himself with what he needed.

His sweet child had been born while this was occurring and Bill had such sadness because he could not be with his daughter. He still had that inborn goodness, so he paid child support out of his check when he didn't have to. His ex-wife was wealthy due to her parents and was making out fine. The duty and love he felt for his child rose above his disabling disease.

Bill eventually moved to MO with my aunt and uncle. They let him have his own trailer in a park where they had a mobile for themselves to retire. After a number of years his dad died, and a year later Bill died. Of what did he die? Well no one said, but without a doubt he died from his mental disorder. It was a long slow death and his body gave up, so at 48 years of age he left us while in the hospital. His sister and I were with him and when he passed, I was grateful that now he was at peace and in God's hands.

Today Bill would have a much better outlook due to the advancement in medicines and more. I am writing this to tell Bill's story but also to let the people with a brain disorder know that once so bad, now so much better with the help of the medications today and support groups and doctors and more that recognize that mental illness is a disease of the brain.

We can't bring Bill back, but we can remember him and honor his memory knowing that Bill was not his disease; he was always still sweet wonderful Bill who had a brain disorder called schizophrenia. Bill was not the disease.

I love you Bill and miss you,
Rene

MY PERSONAL BATTLES WITH MEDICATIONS

By Irene Marshall

I have strong feelings on the subject of medications. As a young girl of 14 years of age I was diagnosed with General Anxiety Disorder. I was told by the doctors I must take the tranquilizers they prescribed. Because of the stigma, I felt less than the others having to take medication but the doctors insisted. I took myself off the prescription at age 16, 2 years later.

At age 24 I went into full blown panic attacks and became almost homebound. The doctors once again told me I had to take tranquilizers...Now they went as far as to state, "If you don't you'll die of high blood pressure or heart disease and it won't take long with your anxiety level." I took them.

At age 45 I was told by a doctor, "You can no longer take them; I'm sorry, take extra blood pressure medication." I was frightened and I found a caring doctor who said he'd give them to me. Once again I felt less than worthy.

Today I don't need them very much but still get my prescription filled. If my doctor fully retires I could be an older woman in trouble.

I feel the knowledge of the medication given to us with the advice that goes with it should be carefully worded. The medical world needs to come together with brain disorders and know we are not addicts...the stigma still survives, especially on tranquilizers.

My prayer is to all who take medications for their brain disorder to constantly keep their doctors updated on what they need and how they feel.

We must keep making progress, all of us together. We must be informed about the medicines we take and make our decisions with the doctor how they are working for us.

Never give up hope,
Irene Marshall

BEN WRIGHT

I was born in 1956. My mother was a very mean woman, but my father was kind and supportive. Alone he raised my 3 brothers, my 3 sisters and me! My dad died in 2002.

I got married in 1985, but my wife and I divorced 2 weeks later, when I couldn't tolerate the drug environment any more. My step-daughter and I have kept in touch.

I've lived in Joplin since 2001. At one time I was a licensed program trainer for the mentally challenged. I worked at a plastic industry in Joplin, also.

I've been attending NAMI meetings for around 1 year, and have made some really good friends.

AMANDA

My childhood was plagued by my being molested by 3 people. Even today, I have changed counselors whenever we start to discuss this "touchy subject." I have more than a little trouble talking about that!

A bi-sexual partner of mine was raped and murdered in 1996; this was also very painful.

I only had a few friends during my childhood. It was really pretty much a lonely time for me.

I discovered NAMI 18 months ago, and I feel it was a blessing sent from God! During these months, I've made several friends like Alex, (a young man who facilitates at NAMI meetings) Sheryl and Mark, the two latter folks who live also in Neosho. NAMI has been a lifesaver- it's so nice to meet people who share common experiences like mine. It's prevented a tragic outcome in my life, as when I was considering suicide one week, NAMI folks saw

I would be admitted for psychiatric help. Since that time period, I've seen I have so much to live for!!

My diagnosis is bi-polar2, PTSD, generalized anxiety, and borderline personality disorder.

I was admitted to a psychiatric ward recently during my walk with mental illness, and it really turn out to be a positive experience! The doctors and nurses there really did listen to me, and I got a fresh start with meds and counselors' sessions, too.

I helped my mom awhile back during a serious episode in her life.

My fiancé and I plan to marry soon-he now has a good job and is kind and supportive of me. I thank God for Nathan's presence every single day.

Just F.Y.I: While I was in the psychiatric unit, "I went off" on a nurse that commented NAMI wasn't a good place to make friends. I let her know that I'd personally made more than a few friends at NAMI, and she had better re-think her story!

I've got 3 healthy, happy kids, and I love each one of them!

AMANDA'S DAUGHTER IZABELLE

My name is Izabelle and I am 11 years old.

The first time I thought mom had a problem was when she attended a NAMI meeting. Mom explained all about what NAMI was to me, and it impressed me in a positive way! I was 9 ½ years old at that time.

We still have ups and downs relating to mom's illness, but she is learning to cope, while going often to her weekly NAMI meetings. Mom is sometimes moody, and we do argue about things occasionally.

We do talk about mental illness at times, and I always feel better when we do. I try to keep a regular routine, and I feel this helps mom's outlook around our home.

I've gone to a number of NAMI activities with mom, and the members always made me feel welcome.

My younger sister Charlotte, who is 7, is really too young to know about mental illness. She did come to a game night at NAMI once. She said she had a good time.

If it wasn't for mom's NAMI support group, she wouldn't feel nearly as well as she does. NAMI really helps my mom!

SANDEE ABLE

I had never heard the phrase "mental illness" until I was 16 years old and I saw my first therapist. I was pretty sure that there was something wrong with me, as I didn't act or think like the people who surrounded me.

On top of my old problems, I was facing a whole new set of problems as I was in an entire new location with a different set of people than who I grew up with! I knew that if I was going to make it, I was going to have to adapt to a whole new life, which I was willing to try, although there were some very real obstacles in my way.

The first thing in my way was culture shock, as I'd come from the city of Spokane, Washington. Now I was living in the county of Kalvesta way out in western Kansas. In Spokane, I knew who and what I should be afraid of, but in Kansas I was facing a new type of fear. I had no security and I was all alone. It wasn't long until I became my own worst enemy.

I began having nightmares day and night, which the therapist called "flashbacks". I could not get my mind to shut off. I kept going through physical abuse and sexual abuse, day after day and night after night. My therapist called this "PTSD". They also put it in my records that I had major depression with major anxiety. I had my first suicide attempt at age 18 when I drank some cleaner that was under the kitchen sink which was at my aunt and uncle's house where I was staying.

No one could see that I just wanted my mind to shut off. I couldn't escape the thoughts that were circulating in my head. It was clear that the uncle and aunt I was living with were not helping the problem. I lived in total chaos the next 4 years until graduating from high school.

I started seeing another therapist when I was 21 following my second suicide attempt. I was just living from therapist appointment to therapist appointment. I was just waiting for these therapists to fix everything, to make the pain leave. In 1993 I began seeing a therapist who gave me some information that changed everything for me.

I came to an understanding of what and how I was thinking about things. This new therapist said something I had never heard before. "Expectations are appointments for disappointments."

All that time I was expecting the therapists to have the answers I needed and wanted to have a different life. I finally heard that what I was dealing with from my past could not be cured, but that with the right types of medications and continuing with my therapy that I was doing to learn how to cope with my life. I would be able to live my life in a different way and that maybe one day I might find contentment and peace, but it was going to be a long, hard road, and that it wouldn't happen overnight. I tried and tried many medications over the years.

I was also drinking and experimenting with other drugs beside what were prescribed to me, convincing myself that "more was better." I could hold jobs, thinking they were good for my condition, not knowing I was causing myself more problems with the law, and then being committed to the state mental hospital in my late 20's.

This experience didn't help my mental condition whatsoever. Finally, someone told me that things wouldn't get better until I would change what I was doing. The fact was that I was the one who would have to make these changes. My life stayed in chaos and confusion mentally for the next several years. Labor Day of 2000 was the last day I worked in the nursing field. I had my last suicide attempt that day.

It took 3 rescue units and a lifeline helicopter to save me and bring me back, as I'd taken 700 pills and I was basically dead. But it was a God thing that I came out of that overdose with the clarity of mind that I had. My life just was not the same, but the words I'd heard before registered with me. Then on 2-18-02 I made the decision to make the changes I needed to make. I waited until my husband went into a different part of the house. Then I took my car and drove off. As I drove down the Interstate I saw a sign saying "Joplin" so I turned around, drove back to it and stopped at a convenience store for a soda and some gas.

There were 3 girls in the store talking about the Lafayette House, so I asked them about it and they told me where it was. I went there and walked inside. I checked it out and there was a bed there so I took it. My first few days there were not fun. I began going through withdrawals from the alcohol and drugs that I'd been taking, and this lasted 2 weeks. I made a promise I would never go through that again. I was going to groups on self-esteem, and groups on finding out who I was.

I began going to Narcotics Anonymous and got a sponsor and started writing steps and doing service work while staying clean. After 1 year of being clean, the flashbacks started up again and I didn't know why. I started back in therapy again and realized that I had to work on my mental stuff as well as having to stay clean, or that I would have the same conflict with one or the other. When I had 5 years clean, it came back to me in a meeting that because I was taking meds for my mental stuff, that I had lost my clean time. I freaked!

Without taking care of both of these conditions I wasn't going to make it in life. I can't have one without the other. Several people don't understand that I have a brain disorder-I'm not crazy, but all the time I've been medicated I've not been in a psych unit or in jail. I have 12 years clean. I am not financially well off but the serenity and stability that

I have in my life today, I wouldn't give up for any price. I have my life back today, and I am at peace with Sandee.

THANK YOU
Sandee Able

JENNIFER

My psychosis began around age 11 or so, when my father passed away. My emotions were getting the best of me. I hated everyone in the world, and truly wished I could kill people although I'd never before been a violent girl.

Around age 15 or so, I was admitted to Juvenile Detention in California. I was diagnosed as having bi-polar condition.

In my 20's I really struggled with mental illness, as I would wander around in the night, and suffered from hearing voices and hallucinating a lot.

I recall entering a hospital a few times, when I'd become comatose.

Today, I take my meds, enjoy my mom and step-dad, my church, and listening to Gospel music quite often.

ALEX

When I was 15 years old, I was diagnosed as having depression. At 18 the diagnosis was bi-polar 1, and at 19, my mental condition became schizophrenic. When asked about my illness, I just say, "I'm schizophrenic."

When I was 17, I attempted suicide, canceling any hopes of the wrestling career I'd hoped to enjoy at Joplin High School.

Around this time period, I was admitted to a facility at Springfield, MO for examinations. I lost 10 pounds in a week while there, as I refused to eat.

A medication I was on, Risperdal, made me gain 100 pounds! Then I went on Seroquel 50 mg., where I maintained my weight, and finally I've taken Clozaril and I've lost 100 pounds.

I've often suffered with hallucinations, (I've seen "the cat in the hat"), and I've heard a lot of fearful voices, too.

I got violent in an instance which occurred October 14, 2005. It took 20 security guards to contain me!

I've attended NAMI for 2 years, and I've gotten some relief from our group. I've participated in 2 NAMI walks in the springtime.

I volunteer at Joplin Freeman hospital, transporting people there, in the hospital. A doctor told me my hallucinations would gradually improve with time.

I am a facilitator at our weekly NAMI group.

MARCUS

My journey with mental illness started at the young age of 18, when I should've been looking ahead at life with excitement. Instead, a roller coaster ride of psychosis and fear were my lot!

My family and I were devastated by these happenings, but no answers seemed available.

One year later, I was admitted to a rehabilitation center near K.C., MO. I began a regimen of meds that really just made me numb, but at that time that was all that were available. But today, thank the Good Lord there are several excellent anti-psychotic drugs and I am convinced that the effort to find "the right drugs" for us is paramount in our road toward recovery!

As I tried to lead a normal life, it soon became obvious that probably wasn't going to happen real soon. I did work at my family's grocery store, but often had to leave early, as I just couldn't handle the anxiety attacks. My folks and family were very good to me during this rough period of time; my father, a man I today idolize, drove me to K.C. every 3 weeks to visit my psychiatrist.

In 1979 I met and married my first wife, and we have 2 children. These kids are both thriving in young adulthood, and are a blessing to the many lives they touch! My wife helped me return to God, and today I'm blessed in our local church's ministries.

A few years into our marriage I stopped taking my meds, as I was convinced God had healed me of my illness. This certainly didn't turn out positive, and I divorced my wife and hurt many in my family. I finally did come to my senses, started a couple of new meds, got a job, found a new counselor, and attended a church for emotional and spiritual support. It was then I married once more, and Rose and I've seen our 18th anniversary recently! Our marriage has been very rewarding and hopefully shall continue to thrive.

NAMI Joplin has been a huge support to me since I joined the group three years ago. Our group is a unique group of folks committed to each other's needs. I enjoy, along with our group the feedback and encouragement given by all every Tuesday night. An awesome event, that occurs every Tuesday night, is whenever one or more members arrive feeling down and out, then we other members jump up to help these people leave the meeting feeling encouraged and hopeful once again! It's amazing, and is exactly what a support group should be.

Today, by the grace of God and by many people's support, I hold down a full-time position in our dairy department at our Wal-Mart SuperCenter, teach Sunday School beside 3 other teachers, give music lessons to several fine students, and get a huge kick from going to NAMI meetings every week! I'm very blessed and enjoy a full life!

If there is a message I can pass on, it would be that there is HOPE! Seek out knowledge and make a plan for recovery with fellow members. Tomorrow really can be a brighter day for us!

AMANDA, MARCUS' DAUGHTER

The first time that I noticed my dad had a problem was about the time I was in the 6th grade. He acted different and my mom and he fought more.

Things got more heated at home, and one tough day my dad moved out. Mom told us my dad "was sick."

Some of my dad's friends were of questionable origins and my mom and my brother and I lived in a cloud of fear for awhile.

The church that my mom and brother and I attended asked us to leave, which was stressful!

There were days that dad just wasn't making a lot of sense, like when he repeated questions; it appeared his medications were just not working well.

Whenever dad began taking his newer, better drugs, he acted more like the man we once knew.

It's really good to have a healthier dad nowadays!

PHILLIP, MARCUS' SON

I was only around 7 or so years old when my dad had "problems". He and mom divorced at the same time, which just compounded the stresses. I was pretty sure that my dad's getting off his med's was the main cause for our problems. We visited dad once weekly with my grandpa and grandma present. This helped our relationships to continue even though dad wasn't 100% mentally.

These past several years has seen a stronger dad for us to enjoy, and it's really great to know that he takes his meds religiously!

CHERIE

It started with the suicide of my brother, Russell on Sept. 12, 2010. That's when my world fell apart and everything came crashing in around me. My name is Cherie and this is the story about how mental illness has affected my life.

I am a stuffer of emotions. That began at an early age for me. I was molested from the age of 9-12 by my brother. It didn't end til we thought I might be pregnant. It was then he told mom. She acquired a test, which I took and it was negative. I was told, "Never do that again!" There wasn't any punishment for my brother. That began decades of stuffing emotions and feeling worthless.

When I was 16, I was date raped. I never told it to anyone; I just figured it didn't matter because I was already so damaged. Once again, I stuffed it down. I sang in a Gospel group with my dad, and we took a number of long trips on a bus with the band. One member of the group took advantage of me on one of those trips. I thought he was just being nice to me by talking to me and holding my hands. Then came a foot massage. Then he began sucking on my toes, provoking a response in me that I was incredibly ashamed of. I just knew I would ruin the trip if I told anyone so again I stuffed it.

There are other instances like this that have happened. It seemed I just couldn't get far enough away from people. After the date rape when I was 16, I attempted suicide by cutting my wrist. It was not a good attempt. An attempt I was able to hide from everyone and never tell anyone about. It was after that I decided to build a large fortress of walls around my emotions and never let anyone in again.

Hiding and stuffing my emotions worked until that terrible Friday in September. No matter how hard I tried I could no longer keep my emotions in check any longer. I fell into a deep depression with high anxiety and PTSD right along with it. Once the emotions began flowing out, I wanted to hide from everybody. I began isolating and trying to come up with reasons and excuses not to go anywhere or be with people. The self-harm and suicidal thoughts in my head got harder and harder to control. I finally told my husband and he didn't know how to handle me either.

I have been in and out of hospitals about 5 times over the past 5 years. I always go willingly as I keep thinking someday the doctors will get the right medicine combination for me and I will be better. After my last stay in the hospital, I wanted to find something that could keep me more grounded. I wanted to be able to talk to people who understood how I felt without judging my actions or feelings, That's when I found NAMI.

I've been attending NAMI meetings since September, 2013. It's nice to have people who care about you, and know how you feel. People who know what it feels like to have a panic attack. Friends who understand when you just break down and cry because you are tired of taking medicine. A group that after you attend one time, you feel like you are a part of another family. NAMI helps you keep it real and they share your issues.

If it wasn't for a super husband, a great therapist and my good friends at NAMI, I would be spending more time at that hospital. I am so thankful for finding people who care.

ROCKY

My psychiatrist urged me to attend NAMI meetings. I go to NAMI for emotional support. I have gone to our Joplin NAMI group for about two or more years.

I was born in Denver, Colorado on July 20, 1948. We moved occasionally to Grandview, and then Belton, MO. before moving to Joplin, MO.

My father was an alcoholic which made life almost unbearable.

I'm taking four medications for depression, which aren't working real well.

I have an older sister and a younger brother.

My father died of suicide when I was around 18.

I married my wife about 35 years ago. We met together at church.

I began seeing a psychiatrist sometime after we

married. I worked as a security guard and eventually went on disability.

CINDY

My life really begins at the age of 13, as my father always seemed to be picking at me. As our strong personalities would clash; he would push me around and I would push back. I remember there were times when mom would have to step in to keep him from hurting me! This is around the time my Borderline Personality Disorder started to show through. At this young age I began cutting on myself. I would pick up a piece of glass and begin cutting on the palm of my hand. The pain made me feel better, and watching the blood flow made me less anxious. Not only did I cut but I discovered alcohol; whiskey became a regular drink. I would finish off a cantor and then fill it up with water. My parents never said a word, at all!

In order to lighten the burden my mom carried of raising 3 kids on her own, I married. I was only

16. Just three days into our marriage I discovered I'd married a drug addict, and for the next ten years I was subjected to abuse-emotionally, physically, and sexually. My husband had me believing that I couldn't live without him, nor could I support my two young boys.

At the age of 25, I was hospitalized for a cut on my arm and finally received the diagnosis of Borderline Personality Disorder along with Bipolar. I found the strength to divorce my husband and move on with my life. For the next ten years I was in and out of State hospitals.

Learning to live with BLPD and some of my experiences made me find that I got so upset with things that went on with some of my relationships! I stuffed down the pain. But, once again I would cut myself and watching the blood flow would lessen the pressure inside of me.

About 2 or 3 years ago, I found NAMI. It became a safe place where people were there I could relate to. I can bounce ideas off of them and reach out to others with mental illness just like me.

I now have a second family in NAMI, with members I can rely on, another shoulder to cry on, and now I can talk about my pain instead of internalizing it!

SUZANNE HELENE

I was born in 1959. My mom's genealogy went as follows: Monseer, Hollingsworth, Baumgardner, Alwood, Holsinger, Martin, Delaney, & Barnstart.

I lost my mother in 2003. She told me she was very glad there was hope and medications for me. She wondered how much of my mental illness came from my birth on. I was severely premature- I was born at only 6 months gestation.

I couldn't bear being held yet, and I was kept alive in a plastic incubator. Once I could be held, I was taken home. Early photos show me being fed sugar/glucose through my right middle toe. The scar remained 'til my 50's.

As a baby, I could not be given vaccinations; so as a result, I got sick with one type of measles, mumps, chicken pox, and every cold would affect me so much that I couldn't see or smell very well. I also regularly got pneumonia as a baby. I recall my daddy putting aspirins down my throat.

Whenever I was 10 years of age, at Christmas I got a whole bunch of doll furniture. But, (as usual) I was sick and had to stay in bed. I was MAD!!! Crazy mad! At 54, I just now am realizing I do that.

At age 16, and in grade 10, I finally learned to sneak by mom and dad and attend school even if I was ill. Actually, I received an attendance award for missing less than 3 days that year!

I met Laurie's father at Senior Homecoming Dance in 1977. I miscarried my first baby in 1978 when my parents moved me from a secretary position at the beach to Burly, Idaho. They hoped I'd meet some nice Mormon man, which I did, but I returned to Washington (the state) to break up in person. Instead, I became pregnant again. After 4 months, he got arrested as a sex offender.

I had to raise Laurie alone until we met Billy, Jean's father. Laurie would sleep on his demand, and she knew him as her only daddy.

Returning to my life- when pregnant with BJ, I would drink a gallon of milk a day. With Laurie it was strawberry yogurt. Later I learned I would talk to the TV as "baby", as I had seen my grandpa do the same.

As heredity goes, both grandparents were OCD people. They would pick up dust off the floor so they didn't have to use the vacuum cleaner. Gram would use her OCD to eat oleo, and gram-pa would eat butter. Gram sewed my wardrobe twice a year and she taught me to keep my hands busy with needlework and crafts. I took sewing at school, and

I used Mom's sewing machine.

Dad's father committed suicide in 1972. He'd gotten on 20 meds and was seriously depressed after losing dad's mom in separation.

I work at a Cleaning Company in Joplin. I saw a therapist in Neosho through the Center who didn't think I was truly schizophrenic. I'd been having panic attacks frequently as well. Throughout my high school days and before, people said I would jump at my own shadow! Later, I grew out of my shell.

My daughter ended up in foster care twice, and then also ended up with my parents occasionally. Our daughter ended up with a friend's family for a month.

I've made the road to recovery a reality. In 1993, with the help of local professionals, I lost my "secret voices/friends". Today, I'm employed and active as a facilitator at our NAMI chapter.

SCOTT

I was born on April 24, 1964 in Joplin, MO. After growing older I lived in Jefferson City for 5 years. Later, I moved to Kansas City where I lived for 10 years. I was a computer programmer there.

I was fired from my job in K.C. and felt very lucky to have a home to return to in Joplin!

I have been a member of NAMI for 6 years, where I attend weekly meetings. My parents, Rick and Carol are members of the NAMI Board. My dad organizes the yearly NAMI golf tournament every fall. I help out at the tournament as well.

I have 3 brothers and 2 sisters, and 15 nieces and nephews!

GEOFF JEFFERS

My diagnosis of depression & anxiety with paranoia came when I was 24 years old, 25 years ago. My psychiatrist prescribed Stelazine, which seemed to help.

I enjoyed carpentry by trade for 12 years.

My wife, Beth and I married when I turned 34 years old. We have two adopted children; a boy from Romania whom we named Josiah. He was 1 year old when we adopted him. His sister, Olivia comes from China, and was also 1 year old when we adopted her.

My wife works at the Joplin jail.

I lost my job 2 years ago, which made things stressful for my family. I am now working part-time cutting firewood.

I've been attending NAMI meetings for 3 months now, and I enjoy the openness we share.

These past 3 years my condition has worsened. I struggle daily with my depression, but I just take life one day at a time.

SHARYL GOODING

I'll begin my story saying I was born in Webb City, MO., and I lived there from 1959 'til 1992. My childhood was mostly upbeat. I had an identical twin whom I've not ever met!

My mom died 2 days after Christmas in 2003, and my husband died one week later in 2004. I was admitted in a psychiatric ward in Joplin in 2004-it helped me, and I feel I made lots of progress there!

Joplin NAMI has really given me hope, and I look forward to our weekly meetings with anticipation.

I exercise by swimming at the Y in Joplin, and I exercise at other facilities as well. In 2008, I moved to Michigan Street and enjoyed living there. My cat, Kali & I play together a lot, which brings me joy.

An art teacher with an organization here gave

me some art material which I'm enjoying. I'm hoping to be among friends at NAMI in the future.

I attend church each Sunday and Thursday. I also enjoy playing piano & guitar.

NAMI has given me more friends than even my own neighborhood friends!

HOPE

My life in this world began on November 17, 1949. I was born and raised in Joplin. I have two brothers and one sister.

My dad held down a variety of jobs and also preached the Gospel part of the time. My family attended church faithfully and rarely missed a service.

I was traumatized at age 19 when I was raped, and then raped again at age 20. I barely survived the last attack, taking quite awhile for my recovery!

I was diagnosed at age 30 as having schizophrenia. My mother explained it to me as my "just not being Christian". I received medicines for my mental conditions, (schizophrenia and PTSD). In 1980 my mother had me admitted to an institution. This was the start of my being in and out of mental institutions over a period of several years.

My experience with NAMI has been a blessing. The people in our group are upbeat, and we discuss interesting topics during our weekly meetings. I've been a part of our NAMI group for around 6 months and enjoy all the fellowship!

NATHAN

Whenever I was 12 years old, my folks divorced and my dad got custody of me. It was around 1994 and I lived in Joplin at the time.

My dad put me in and out of mental hospitals, and I recall that at one of them I was given a thorough exam, and I benefited from it! I was diagnosed with PTSD, Borderline Personality Disorder, and Paranoid Schizophrenia. I was given Zoloft which worked well.

I was entered into the Learning Disability program at my school in Junior High and High School which were functioning at a 2nd grade level. Whenever I was 17 years old, a police detective friend saw that my home environment wasn't healthy for me, and I moved out of my dad's home.

When I turned 24, I decided to move to Salt Lake City and worked with the Job Corps! This certainly was a big boost to my outlook on life! A doctor I was seeing prescribed Zoloft and Wellbutrin, although I still felt periods of anxiety. One day, I had a four hour anxiety attack, and then I felt God spoke to my heart saying, *Why are you doing this to yourself?* At that moment, I decided to never let my emotions determine how I acted!

Following working at Job Corps, and while still in Salt Lake City I bought a home. But soon after, I lost the home to the woman I had been living with! This caused me to have a very bad reaction to all of this stress. I became suicidal, and actually wished the police would shoot me and put me out of my misery! I overdosed a number of times, when I realized that my dying was God's business and not mine.

Later on, I moved to Bentonville, Arkansas where the case worker I was seeing took me off my medicine. Today, I'm still off my meds, although I do feel anxious at times.

I have noticed lots of improvement in my fiancée since she joined NAMI.

COMMONLY KNOWN MENTAL ILLNESSES

Schizophrenia

Schizophrenia is a serious mental illness that affects 2.4 million American adults over the age of 18. Although it affects men and women with equal frequency, schizophrenia most often appears in men in their late teens and early 20's, while it appears in women in their late 20's or early 30's. Finding the causes for schizophrenia proves to be difficult as the cause and course of the illness is unique for each individual.

Interfering with a person's ability to think clearly, manage emotions, make decisions and relate to others, schizophrenia impairs a person's ability to function to their potential when it is not treated. Unfortunately, no single source of treatment exists. Research has linked schizophrenia to a multitude of possible causes, including aspects of brain chemistry and structure as well as environmental causes.

Schizo-Affective Disorder

Schizo-affective disorder is a serious mental illness that affects about 1 in 100 people. Schizo-affective disorder as a diagnostic entity has features that resemble both schizophrenia and also serious mood (affective) symptoms. Many of the strategies used to treat both schizophrenia and affective conditions can be employed for this condition. These include both anti-psychotic and mood stabilizing medications, family involvement, psychosocial strategies, self-care, peer support, psychotherapy and integrated care for co-occurring substance (when appropriate) .

A person that has schizo-affective disorder will experience delusions, hallucinations, other systems that are characteristic of schizophrenia and significant disturbances in their mood (affective symptoms). According to the DSM-IV-TR, people who experience more than two weeks of psychotic symptoms in the absence of severe mood disturbances, and then have symptoms of either depression or bipolar disorder-may have schizo-affective disorder.

Schizo-affective disorder is thought to be between the bipolar and schizophrenia diagnosis as it has the features of both.

Depression

Clinical depression is more than having a bad day or coping with a major loss such as the death of a parent, grandparent, or even a favorite pet. It also isn't a personal weakness or character flaw. It is a brain disorder that affects the whole person, it affects the way one feels, thinks, and acts.

Some common signs of depression include:

Persistent sadness and hopelessness

Increased irritability or agitation

Changes in eating or sleeping habits

Indecision, lack of concentration, or forgetfulness

Poor self-esteem or guilt

Frequent physical complaints such as headaches or stomachaches

Drug &/or alcohol abuse and

Thoughts of death or suicide

Fortunately, the prognosis for depression is good. Once diagnosed, medication and psycho-therapy can effectively treat 80% of clinically depressed individuals.

Bipolar Disorder (Manic Depression)

People living with bipolar depression experience periods of severe highs (mania) and severe lows (depression). Hyperactivity, impulsiveness, increased sex drive, exaggerated feelings of self-confidence, and loss of control, characterize the mania. It is often described as one's best feeling ever, so people often fail to seek treatment during this phase. The depressive phase is characterized by extreme sadness and hopelessness, low self-esteem and thoughts of suicide. These moods swing from one to the other, and they may last days, weeks, or months. They are often separated by periods of fairly normal moods. Evidence suggests the cause may be a chemical imbalance in the brain, though a major life change, or serious loss can trigger an episode. Treatment is successful in 80% or 90% of all cases depending on individual response to treatment.

Anxiety Disorders

Some people experience feeling anxious much of the time-sometimes getting in the way of daily activities or schedules. These people are going through anxiety disorders. There are several different types:

Panic disorder causes recurring and unexpected panic attacks, instances of extreme fear or discomfort that start abruptly and build to a rapid peak, usually within ten minutes. Panic attacks are characterized by heart palpitations, sweating, trembling, shortness of breath, chest pain, the sensation of choking, nausea, dizziness, fear of losing control or dying, chills and/or hot flashes.

Additionally, panic attacks are usually accompanied by a sense of looming danger and a strong desire to escape. Panic disorder is diagnosed more often in women than men, and is mostly occurring between late adolescence and mid 30's.

Obsessive Compulsive Disorder (OCD) is known for people's intrusive and inappropriate thoughts that run constantly through one's mind (obsessions) and repetitive behaviors that someone feels they must do (compulsions). Common obsessions include fear of contamination, fixation on lucky or unlucky numbers, fear of danger to oneself or others, and need for exactness. The most common compulsions include ritualistic hand washing, counting, checking, hoarding, and arranging. Equally common in males and females, OCD often appears earlier in males.

Post-Traumatic Stress Disorder (PTSD) is an intense illness caused by one personally experiencing or witnessing a violent or tragic event that can result in feelings of intense fear, helplessness, or horror. Events that can lead up to this anxiety disorder include rape, war, natural disasters, abuse and serious accidents. Sometimes people experience nightmares, hallucinations, or flashbacks over and over.

Individuals with General Anxiety Disorder (GAD) experience excessive anxiety and worry about everyday events and/or activities. Physical symptoms include edginess, fatigue, difficulty concentrating, irritability, muscle tension, and sleep disturbances. To be diagnosed one must experience this anxiety for most days during a period of six months or longer.

MAKE TIME FOR LEISURE ACTIVITIES AND REST

As important as activity is, it's equally important to relax and rest.

Hobbies: Hobbies can be a good source of relaxation and personal fulfillment. It's important to find activities and hobbies that are interesting and rewarding.

Sleep: Regular sleep patterns are significant. When sleep routines vary, maintaining wellness becomes difficult.

Support System: A good support system is essential to sustaining recovery. Socializing with other people who are experiencing the same challenges can be positively reinforcing. You may find these people in community support groups or drop-in centers. Also look for other NAMI consumer support and education programs like peer to peer, NAMI care, and Hearts & Minds. Recovery is not a solo project.

SUCCESSES – HOPES – DREAMS

Before developing a mental illness, consumers came from different backgrounds, had a variety of skills and ambitions, and approached life in their own particular ways. One key to recovery is remembering each person is unique and has his or her own needs and desires.

However, certain aspects of recovery are common to all people who have brain disorders. Accepting the illness, taking daily medication as prescribed, and using coping strategies for managing stress are basic steps that provide the foundation for moving forward and accomplishing personal goals.

Start small and build on early successes. Set realistic, attainable goals. In the beginning it may be very important to learn how to handle daily tasks such as shopping, cooking, laundry, and cleaning up your living environment. Later you'll be able to add a wider range of activities. As you feel better, you can think about volunteer work, a regular job, going to school, or other major goals. Break larger goals into smaller more manageable ones. Accomplishing one goal will give you confidence to go on to the next.

Set personal goals while pursuing your dreams. It's important for each person to figure out what he or she really wants from life. Each individual must determine what constitutes personal success. Consumers should value dreams and the opportunity to work toward them, just as they did before they became ill.

Due to acceptance and treatment of their illnesses, many people may discover new interests.

Recovery doesn't happen overnight. Even if there are setbacks, and discouragement sets in, determination to stay as healthy as possible will help you progress toward accomplishing the things in life that are the most personally meaningful!

MENTAL ILLNESS: THE CAUSES

Imbalance of brain chemicals. No one knows the exact causes of severe mental illnesses but scientific evidence suggests they're a result- or at least in good part- of chemical imbalances in the brain.

Genetics-Genes: The proteins inside our cells with information we pass from one generation to another- seem to play a role in many mental illnesses. Families will often see similar symptoms in offspring or remember them from grandparents. Some people inherit, through their genes, a tendency to develop these illnesses.

Life Events: Life events, such as a serious loss, trauma, chronic illness, a difficult relationship, or financial problems might trigger the beginning of a mental illness. Chronic stress and/or abuse can also cause the onset of these illnesses in people who have a predisposition to them, but it is important to know and remember that poor upbringing or "personality defects" do not cause these illnesses.

No One Is To Blame!

Having a mental illness does not mean there is anything adherently wrong with you. Having a brain disorder does not affect your worth as a human being or encapsulate who you are any more than being diabetic would.

In spite of their illnesses, all people are valuable and have much to offer others. Some of the most courageous people in the world are those who are living daily with the realities of having a brain disorder. They and their families should be looked upon for wisdom and guidance.

THE PURPOSE OF MEDICATIONS IN TREATING MENTAL ILLNESS

If you have a heart disorder, you take medication. If you have diabetes, you take insulin. It's a very common thing. This is an honest, matter of fact approach to the need for medicine. A similar approach can be applied when treating mental illness. Since there is no cure for mental illness, the goals of medical treatment are to:

-Eliminate or reduce symptoms

-Minimize side effects of medications

-Prevent relapse and hospitalizations

-Enable people with these illnesses to resume social, work, and school activities.

Because serious mental illnesses are primarily disorders involving brain chemistry, medication is necessary to correct the brain's chemical malfunctioning. Medications are the foundation of treatment and are critical to achieving positive results for people working on recovery.

Additional treatments and coping skills can help consumers manage their illnesses. However, if taking the right medication(s) at the right dosage consistently is not part of your treatment plan, other attempts to deal effectively with mental illness may not be enough to keep you healthy.

THINGS TO THINK ABOUT

We must trust God for the future! He can see ahead of us and prepare us for what might be coming into our lives.

Today is really all we've got; tomorrow will surely have its own problems.

We mustn't miss today's blessings while worrying about tomorrow!

A HIGHER QUALITY OF LIFE

Here is a list of a few items that can really aid mentally ill folks towards achieving a higher quality of life.

Find a nurse practitioner or psychiatrist that will prescribe medicines for us. Try the medicines your doctor prescribes, until finding the "right ones." This may take a while, but it's essential in our road to recovery!

Get plenty of rest. Our bodies run better when we'll do this. Try to eat and drink the healthy foods available to us. It's a great goal to have.

Join a support group. (Why not NAMI)

Try finding a local church or spiritual group where you can find God's presence and healing powers. We gain real strength by doing this!

Try to find a hobby: Maybe take some music lessons or an art class.

COPING STRATEGIES

The reality of having a severe mental illness means that a complete treatment program must be developed and followed carefully and consistently. Wellness can be maintained only when you include coping skills as an integral part of that plan. These coping skills are beneficial to anyone that has a mental illness.

Missouri NAMI Programs

NAMI Basics
NAMI Family to Family
NAMI Peer to Peer
NAMI Connection Recovery Support Group
NAMI Family Support Group
NAMI Parents and Teachers as Allies
NAMI Walks

NAMI Sharing Hope
NAMI in Our Own Voice Programmer
NAMI Hearts and Minds
NAMI on Campus
NAMI Provider Education

REFERENCES

All References are NAMI Sources

NAMI Magazine: In Our Own Voice; Living with mental illness

Depression
Bipolar Disorder, (Manic Depression)
Schizophrenia
Anxiety Disorders
Make time for leisure activities and rest
Successes, hopes, dreams
Mental Illness; the Causes
No One Is To Blame
The purpose of medications in treating mental illness
Coping Strategies

Missouri NAMI Website:
NAMI.org/MSTemplate.cfm?MicrositeID=310

Missouri NAMI Programs
Schizo-Affective Disorder

www.ingramcontent.com/pod-product-compliance
Lightning Source LLC
Chambersburg PA
CBHW060532030426
42337CB00021B/4221